Journey back to joy

Rediscovering repentance

Dai Hankey

Journey back to joy

Rediscovering repentance

Dai Hankey

www.uniontheology.org

a division of 10ofthose.com

Copyright © 2017 by Dai Hankey

First published in Great Britain in 2017

British Library Cataloguing in Publication Data
A record for this book is available from the British Library

ISBN: 978-1-911272-81-6

Designed by Steve Devane

Printed in Denmark by Nørhaven

10Publishing, a division of 10ofthose.com

Unit C, Tomlinson Road, Leyland, PR25 2DY, England

Email: info@10ofthose.com

Website: www.10ofthose.com

CONTENTS

Introduction

On Monday 9 July 2001 the Croatian wildcard Goran Ivanisevic defeated Pat Rafter in five epic sets to win the men's Wimbledon championship. It was one of the most memorable matches ever played on Centre Court. The following day Goran returned to his home town, Split, where thousands of rapturous fans welcomed their hero back. This is how the BBC reported it: 'When Goran finally appeared on stage the crowd was euphoric. Smiling and crying for joy they yelled: "Goran, we love you." Initially he simply looked bemused at the adulation, but going with the spirit of the moment he had soon stripped down to his underpants throwing his clothes into the ecstatic crowd.'[1]

Wow! There's joy ... but then there's a whole new level of joy that prompts dancing with the masses in the streets in your underpants! Those iconic scenes in Split were unforgettable – it was truly amazing to see how one man's joy could impact an entire nation, but that's what joy does.

As crazy as it sounds, Goran's homecoming celebrations remind me of the character we will be studying in this little book: King David. More often than not we tend to think of David as the shepherd boy who defeated giant Goliath with a slingshot, and then a warrior poet skilled with sword and harp. But as we begin our journey with King David we find him 'doing a Goran' and dancing through the streets in his underwear:

> David went to bring up the ark of God from the house of Obed-Edom to the City of David with rejoicing. When those who were carrying the ark of the Lord had taken six steps, he sacrificed a bull and a fattened calf. Wearing a linen ephod, David was dancing before the Lord with all his might, while he and all Israel were bringing up the ark of the Lord with shouts and the sound of trumpets (2 Sam. 6:12–15).

Why did David dance? Because after its capture by the Philistines and temporary stay in Kiriath Jearim, the ark of God was finally coming home to Jerusalem, the city of God. It is impossible to overstate the value and significance of this portable, gold-plated chest to the people of Israel. The ark represented the blessed presence of God among His people (Ex. 25:22) so it *really* mattered to them. The arrival of the ark signified that God's glory was returning to Israel. He was once again drawing close to His people. As David famously put it, while addressing God, 'you will fill me with joy in your presence' (Ps. 16:11). Indeed as the ark entered the city, David was so overcome with joy that he simply could not keep it in, so he cut loose, partied hard and all Israel partied with him. The people were sucked into the vortex of David's delight because that's what joy does.

Mercifully we do not need an ark to know the joy of God's presence today; we just need Jesus (aka Immanuel, which means 'God *with* us'). Jesus came to live among us, to die for us and to rise again in order that we might have life, abundant and eternal. He came to save us. No wonder the angel announced His birth as 'good news that will cause great joy for all the people' (Luke 2:10). Furthermore, by the power of the Holy Spirit who indwells His people, Jesus is able to keep His promise to be forever present with us, even to the end of the age.[2] So if true joy is found in God's presence, then to know Jesus *is* to know joy.

Do you have that joy? If you don't, then my prayerful hope is that this book will help you to attain it, and so to discover and experience first-hand the sweet joy of Jesus. If you do know that joy, then by all means cherish it and revel in it. However, like Han Solo warned Luke Skywalker, 'Don't get cocky!' because, as we are about to learn from King David, it is painfully possible to lose that joy …

Tragedy – sin committed

1

David's journey from humble shepherd boy to King of Israel is heady stuff. The defeat of Goliath might have made him front-page news, but that was only the beginning. In the years that followed, against a backdrop of great hardship and vicious opposition, David's qualities shone through: anointed musician, valiant warrior, shrewd tactician, merciful servant, faithful friend and inspiring leader. He was clearly a man after God's own heart. By the time David had been crowned king and jitterbugged the ark back into Jerusalem, he was both a national hero and a spiritual heavyweight. The Bible chapters which immediately follow the ark's return only enhance that view: stunning military victories and epic grace shown to his former enemy's family, not to mention God's great covenant promise that the Messiah – Jesus Christ – would be born from David's line. *Boom!*

David was at the peak of his powers and the summit of his success. What could possibly go wrong? Cue 2 Samuel 11 …

In the spring, at the time when kings go off to war, David sent Joab out with the king's men and the whole Israelite army. They destroyed the Ammonites and besieged Rabbah. But David remained in Jerusalem.

One evening David got up from his bed and walked around on the roof of the palace. From the roof he saw a woman bathing. The woman was very beautiful, and David sent someone to find out about her. The man said, 'She is Bathsheba, the daughter of Eliam and the wife of Uriah the Hittite.' Then David sent messengers to get her. She came to him, and he slept with her. (Now she was purifying herself from her monthly uncleanness.) Then she went back home. The woman conceived and sent word to David, saying, 'I am pregnant.'

So David sent this word to Joab: 'Send me Uriah the Hittite.' And Joab sent him to David. When Uriah came to him, David asked him how Joab was, how the soldiers were and how the war was going. Then David said to Uriah, 'Go down to your house and wash your feet.' So Uriah left the palace, and a gift from the king was sent after him. But Uriah slept at the entrance to the palace with all his master's servants and did not go down to his house.

David was told, 'Uriah did not go home.' So he asked Uriah, 'Haven't you just come from a military campaign? Why didn't you go home?'

Uriah said to David, 'The ark and Israel and Judah are staying in tents, and my commander Joab and my lord's men are camped in the open country. How could I go to my house to eat and drink and make love to my wife? As surely as you live, I will not do such a thing!'

Then David said to him, 'Stay here one more day, and tomorrow I will send you back.' So Uriah remained in Jerusalem that day and the next. At David's invitation, he ate and drank with him, and David made him drunk. But in the evening Uriah went out to sleep on his mat among his master's servants; he did not go home.

In the morning David wrote a letter to Joab and sent it with Uriah. In it he wrote, 'Put Uriah out in front where the fighting is fiercest. Then withdraw from him so that he will be struck down and die.'

So while Joab had the city under siege, he put Uriah at a place where he knew the strongest defenders were. When the men of the city came out and fought against Joab, some of the men in David's army fell; moreover, Uriah the Hittite died.

Joab sent David a full account of the battle. He instructed the messenger: 'When you have finished giving the king this account of the battle, the king's anger may flare up, and he may ask you, "Why did you get so close to the city to fight? Didn't you know they would shoot arrows from the wall? Who killed Abimelek son of Jerub-Besheth? Didn't a woman drop an upper millstone on him from the wall, so that he died in Thebez? Why did you get so close to the wall?" If he asks you this, then say to him, "Moreover, your servant Uriah the Hittite is dead."'

The messenger set out, and when he arrived he told David everything Joab had sent him to say. The messenger said to David, 'The men overpowered us and came out against us in the open, but we drove them back to the entrance of the city gate. Then the archers shot arrows at your servants from the wall, and some of the king's men died. Moreover, your servant Uriah the Hittite is dead.'

David told the messenger, 'Say this to Joab: "Don't let this upset you; the sword devours one as well as another. Press the attack against the city and destroy it." Say this to encourage Joab.'

When Uriah's wife heard that her husband was dead, she mourned for him. After the time of mourning was over, David had her brought to his house, and she became his wife and bore him a son. But the thing David had done displeased the Lord (2 Sam. 11:1–27).

These verses are as staggering as they are tragic. Is this even the same man?! How could David fall from passionate worshipper to ruthless adulterer and murderous conspirator in such a short space of time? How could he so shamelessly love his God one minute, then so shamefully lust after Uriah's wife the next? While this passage doesn't take us all the way into David's thought process, it does provide a glimpse into what was happening in his heart on that dark, devastating day.

The text tells us that this all played out 'at the time when kings go off to war' (v. 1) – it seems that ancient kings had a war season just like we have a football season. However, David was not where he should have been. The king should have been up front and central at this royal *...as the old saying goes: 'The devil finds work for idle hands.'* rumble, leading his army to yet another victory, but instead he chose the palace above the battlefield and stayed at home – combat boots off, slippers on. Had he got comfortable? Complacent? Cocky, even? Whatever the reason, David was now in grave danger, for as the old saying goes: 'The devil finds work for idle hands.'

David's guard was down and, as he looked out from his palace rooftop one restless evening, he walked straight into the devil's trap. He saw an attractive woman bathing and, rather than bouncing his eyes away and focusing on something, *anything* else, he allowed his thoughts to run wild. Just as the fruit of Eden looked too good to resist, David saw, took and ate the forbidden fruit – though even in his darkest dreams he could not have envisaged the cataclysmic chain of events that this tryst with Bathsheba would trigger. But isn't that just what we do? We choose momentary gratification, regardless of long-term consequences, time and again.

Now, the temptation at this stage would be to look at David's laziness, his dereliction of duty and his roving eye, and conclude that because he was lacking discernment and any meaningful accountability, he made a series of bad decisions. While there may be some truth in that, though, I think this passage points to a much deeper issue …

Upon learning that his adultery had led to an unwanted pregnancy, David quickly sought to cover his tracks. He recalled Bathsheba's husband,

Uriah the Hittite, from the frontline and tried every trick in the book to get him to sleep with his wife, but Uriah just wasn't buying it. Had he clocked that something was going on? Either way, Uriah refused to go home to his wife. His last recorded words reveal as much about where David had gone off the rails as they do about the character of this noble man: 'The ark and Israel and Judah are staying in tents, and my commander Joab and my lord's men are camped in the open country. How could I go to my house to eat and drink and make love to my wife? As surely as you live, I will not do such a thing!' (v. 11).

You have to wonder what happened in the heart and mind of King David as Uriah spoke these words. Surely they cut deep? Even in the midst of fear, pain and confusion, the ark – the symbol of God's glory and His blessed presence among His people – was at the forefront of Uriah's mind. Perhaps the king's worship of God had once rubbed off on him. Maybe he had been present at that unforgettable street party in Jerusalem when his commander-in-chief had cavorted through the streets before the ark, singing, sacrificing and celebrating. But the ark was no longer on David's mind and his passion for God's presence was a distant memory. As for the men of war – those brothers in arms, many of whom had found in David a captain and king to live and die for – Uriah was mindful of them too, but David wasn't.

David gave no thought for the glory of God or the good of his people. David had changed and his wicked actions were merely the overflow of a wayward heart. Before forsaking his army, David had forsaken his God. Before lusting after Bathsheba, David had

Before lusting after Bathsheba, David had stopped loving his Lord.

stopped loving his Lord. This man who had once lost himself in divine joy now found himself at the epicentre of an illicit, murderous affair. The image of King David sending the honourable, mighty Uriah back to the frontline of battle carrying his own death warrant in his hand is beyond harrowing. Little wonder that this chapter closes with the words: 'But the thing David had done displeased the Lord' (v. 27).

How had it come to this? It's easy to speculate, of course, but it's perhaps more important to try to relate. Ask yourself, have you ever capitulated in such a way? I certainly have. My Christian life has been a rollercoaster of soaring highs and sordid lows. Indeed the journey from close, joyful proximity with the Father to feeding with the pigs[3] has sometimes taken just a few mindless moments … or a couple of clicks … or a single catastrophic decision. What about you?

Perhaps you've read this and are feeling more like the Disco Dave of the introduction than the king of carnality in this chapter. If that's you, then take this episode as a warning shot across the bow because if it can happen to David, it *can* happen to you! Or perhaps you've read this and, while you have not plummeted to quite the same depths that David did, you know that your love for God is not what it should be – you have drifted into cold apathy and God seems distant. If that's

… you know that your love for God is not what it should be – you have drifted into cold apathy…

you, then take this as an encouragement to come back from the edge before you fall and to seek the Lord with fresh passion. Start running hard after him again. Or perhaps this chapter paints a picture of where you are at right now? You are trapped in a miserable, stinking pit of your own making and true joy now seems both a distant memory and an impossible dream. Maybe you feel wretched, alone and so far gone, so spiritually numb, that you literally don't care anymore. If that's you, then you have only one hope: grace!

The good news is that God *loves* to give grace to the humble. The bad news is that humility can hurt, as David was about to find out …

Agony –
sin exposed

2

Several years ago I was asked to look after a friend's dog – a large, energetic Dalmatian called Nelson. On the whole Nelson was a good dog, but he did have one significant problem: drool! Nelson was a four-legged slobber machine and no matter how hard you tried to avoid his juicy jowls he'd always get you in the end, as I discovered one humiliating evening in Cardiff. Having been booked to DJ at a nightclub, I strolled into the venue, record box in hand, when people started to laugh at me. The club's UV lighting revealed that ninja Nelson had sneakily drizzled saliva all over my jeans and shirt without my noticing. The spittle stripes, while invisible in daylight, were now shining bright in brilliant white, leaving me looking like something from a low-budget 1980s rock video. It was acutely embarrassing in many ways, but that's what light does – it exposes dirt.

In our last chapter we saw how David had fallen from heights of divine bliss to depths of vile disgrace. Unsurprisingly God was greatly displeased, yet that was not the end of the matter. God was about to lead David on a thrilling journey back to joy. Before the voyage could begin, though, David had to be stopped in his treacherous tracks. God's light was about to shine into David's darkness and expose his dirty secrets:

The LORD sent Nathan to David. When he came to him, he said, 'There were two men in a certain town, one rich and the other poor. The rich man had a very large number of sheep and cattle, but the poor man had nothing except one little ewe lamb he had bought. He raised it, and it grew up with him and his children. It shared his food, drank from his cup and even slept in his arms. It was like a daughter to him.

'Now a traveller came to the rich man, but the rich man refrained from taking one of his own sheep or cattle to prepare a meal for the traveller who had come to him. Instead, he took the ewe lamb that belonged to the poor man and prepared it for the one who had come to him.'

David burned with anger against the man and said to Nathan, 'As surely as the Lord lives, the man who did this must die! He must pay for that lamb four times over, because he did such a thing and had no pity.'

Then Nathan said to David, 'You are the man! This is what the Lord, the God of Israel, says: "I anointed you king over Israel, and I delivered you from the hand of Saul. I gave your master's house to you, and your master's wives into your arms. I gave you all Israel and Judah. And if all this had been too little, I would have given you even more. Why did you despise the word of the Lord by doing what is evil in his eyes? You struck down Uriah the Hittite with the sword and took his wife to be your own. You killed him with the sword of the Ammonites. Now, therefore, the sword shall never depart from your house, because you despised me and took the wife of Uriah the Hittite to be your own."

'This is what the Lord says: "Out of your own household I am going to bring calamity on you.

Before your very eyes I will take your wives and give them to one who is close to you, and he will sleep with your wives in broad daylight. You did it in secret, but I will do this thing in broad daylight before all Israel."'

Then David said to Nathan, 'I have sinned against the LORD.'

Nathan replied, 'The LORD has taken away your sin. You are not going to die. But because by doing this you have shown utter contempt for the LORD, the son born to you will die' (2 Sam. 12:1–14).

You have to take your hat off to Nathan here as confronting a king and telling him that he's a sinner would not have been an easy gig. In fact, had it been Nathan's choice, he probably would have called in sick that day! But this encounter was not Nathan's idea, as the text tells us: 'The LORD sent Nathan to David' (v. 1). By obediently going and faithfully speaking to the king, Nathan teaches us a crucial, life-giving lesson: the darkness which destroys us and robs our joy can be driven back by only one thing – an invasion of God's light. As the psalmist put it: 'The entrance of Your words gives light' (Ps. 119:130, NKJV). To put it another way, without the crucial combo of God's man delivering God's illuminating Word, David would not have turned back to God. His heart would have remained hard, cold and devoid of joy.

Nathan's intervention here might have been #AWKWARD but let's be in no doubt that this divine encounter is absolutely the hinge upon which the door of God's grace to David was going to swing open. If David's relationship with God was ever going to be restored, he was going to need to repent of his sin. David's confession, 'I have sinned against the LORD' (v. 13), only came *after* Nathan had told him straight, 'You are the man!' (v. 7). The prophet's words had laid David's wretched soul bare. That's what light does.

This episode challenges me to the core as it brings to mind the innumerable times that I have deliberately, wilfully turned away from God in reckless rebellion. I wish such times did not exist and despise them but they did … and they still do. It is painful, but necessary, to confess that I struggle every day to live in a way that adequately glorifies the Father or honours the saving sacrifice of His Son or showcases the transformative power of the Holy Spirit. I am gutted that sometimes my life as a follower of Jesus still reeks of my old life as a godless rogue, but if I am going to pass comment on King David's sin and confront you with yours, then it's only appropriate that I hold my hand up and confess my own too. I have lost count of how many times pride, anger, lust and greed have drawn my heart away from Jesus, only to leave me floundering in squalid disgrace. Such seasons have always been marked by acute shame, aching sadness and spiritual numbness.

However, despite knowing deep down that grace, joy and spiritual vitality could only be recovered by returning to God, I have found that the two places I least wanted to be during those times were in God's Word and among His people. Like a cockroach making its home in dingy, darkened cracks, I would avoid the light at all costs, steering

I have found that the two places I least wanted to be...were in God's Word...

clear of any meaningful contact with Christians and relegating my Bible to the role of chief dust collector in the corner of the room. I just wanted to be left alone in my miserable revolt without anything or anyone pricking my dulled conscience. Can you relate to that?

Interestingly, every time that I have turned back to God it was His Word that did the work. Whether it's a piece of Scripture read or recalled, a sermon that managed to penetrate my defences or a friend looking me in the eye and speaking truth straight into my soul, it's the pure beam of biblical truth that gets me *every* time! The beautiful, reassuring message of this passage is that God loves His people too much to leave us floundering in the darkness, even when we, like David, are solely responsible for our sin and utterly deserving of death. As Paul wrote, 'if we are faithless, he remains faithful, for he cannot disown himself' (2 Tim. 2:13). Therefore the God of light[4] sends His people of light[5] to proclaim His Word of light[6] so that our renegade hearts might be arrested by His love and our dark insurgency quashed. This is unfathomable grace and the key to knowing joy restored.

Imagine for a moment what would have happened if the LORD had *not* sent Nathan to speak His Word to David. What would have become of the king? Would he have ever penned Psalm 51? Could he have ever returned to the delirious heights of delight in His God? Mercifully we don't need to speculate because God *did* send Nathan. This was an act of extreme, loving kindness for if God does not confront us with our sin, there is certainly another who will.

Our enemy, Satan, loves nothing more than reminding us of all the times and ways that we've screwed up. Sometimes he hurls charges at us; other times he gently whispers his accusations into our ears. Either way, his motive for speaking to us about our sin is *condemnation* – Satan relishes telling us that we are filthy and guilty as hell, and he delights to leave us wallowing in joyless disgrace and hopeless despair. Conversely, when God speaks to us by His Spirit through His Word, His motive is *conviction* – He too tells us that we are filthy and guilty as hell, but then He leads us to Jesus in whom we find full forgiveness and unparalleled joy.

There is an eternity of difference between the condemnation of the devil and the conviction of the Holy Spirit. Therefore, while Nathan's task was neither easy nor enjoyable, ultimately it was a mission of mercy because God's intention was for David to turn back to Him, to confess his sin and to hear the words: 'The LORD has taken away your sin. You are not going to die' (v. 13). It truly is God's kindness that leads us to repentance.[7]

As you have read this chapter and considered the heart of God, the actions of Nathan and the impact of his words on David, I wonder how it has impacted you. Perhaps it has refreshed your soul and encouraged your heart to be reminded that we have a God who graciously, patiently pursues prodigal children. Maybe you have

Do you have a friend who needs to be lovingly confronted about sin in their life?

been challenged by the ministry of Nathan, a prophet who obediently stepped up to speak God's Word to a king whose heart had strayed from God. Do you have a friend who needs to be lovingly confronted about sin in their life? If so, pray that God would give you wisdom, grace and courage to speak, and that He would grant them a soft heart to listen and to turn back to Him. Alternatively, have you, like David, forsaken your first love, abandoned God and run after the shallow, superficial things of this world? Is it time to open God's Word again with fresh faith, ready to be challenged? Do you need to swallow your pride, face your fears or deal with your wounds as you get plugged into a local church community? Has God's light exposed sinfulness and waywardness in our own heart? If so, do not delay – return to Him today.

Turning back to God requires raw honesty and extraordinary humility and is therefore one of the toughest things to ever do, but it is the only way to expel the darkness and experience grace. Crucially it is also the essential first step on the journey back to joy, as we'll see in the next chapter. And if you need a little help in knowing how to confess your sin and get right with God, you are going to love what's coming next because David wrote a song about it …

Humility –
sin confessed

3

Following his illicit affair with Uriah's wife, the murder of her husband and the consequent confrontation with Nathan the prophet, King David went on to compose a song that stands apart as the ultimate masterpiece on handling shame and regret. It is raw, vulnerable, beautiful and hopeful:

Psalm 51
For the director of music. A psalm of David. When the prophet Nathan came to him after David had committed adultery with Bathsheba.

Have mercy on me, O God,
    according to your unfailing love;
according to your great compassion
    blot out my transgressions.
Wash away all my iniquity
    and cleanse me from my sin.

For I know my transgressions,
    and my sin is always before me.
Against you, you only, have I sinned
    and done what is evil in your sight;
so you are right in your verdict
    and justified when you judge.
Surely I was sinful at birth,
    sinful from the time my mother conceived me.
Yet you desired faithfulness even in the womb;
    you taught me wisdom in that secret place.

Cleanse me with hyssop, and I shall be clean;
    wash me, and I shall be whiter than snow.
Let me hear joy and gladness;
    let the bones you have crushed rejoice.
Hide your face from my sins
    and blot out all my iniquity.

Create in me a pure heart, O God,
    and renew a steadfast spirit within me.
Do not cast me from your presence
    or take your Holy Spirit from me.
Restore to me the joy of your salvation
    and grant me a willing spirit, to sustain me.

Then I will teach transgressors your ways,
    so that sinners will turn back to you.

Deliver me from the guilt of bloodshed, O God,
    you who are God my Saviour,
and my tongue will sing of your righteousness.
    Open my lips, Lord,
and my mouth will declare your praise.
    You do not delight in sacrifice, or I would
        bring it;
    you do not take pleasure in burnt offerings.
My sacrifice, O God, is a broken spirit;
    a broken and contrite heart
    you, God, will not despise.

May it please you to prosper Zion,
    to build up the walls of Jerusalem.
Then you will delight in the sacrifices of
        the righteous,
    in burnt offerings offered whole;
    then bulls will be offered on your altar.

In our previous chapter Nathan had to tell David, 'You are the man!' (2 Sam. 12:7). Psalm 51 is David's way of openly acknowledging 'I am that man!'. The intro alone is mind-blowing: David puts his name to the piece, cites his crime and marks it for the attention of the director of music.[8] In other words the king wanted the full, unedited story of his sinfulness to be expertly recorded and publicly broadcast for all to hear and sing along with it. Imagine a track about your most sordid secrets being recorded by a chart-topping artist and then posted on YouTube!

Such transparency is in itself staggering, but what really sets this song apart is that David's stunning honesty is coupled with steely resolve. He is not content to remain wallowing in self-pity and disgraced despair; rather this song is written with irrepressible faith which in turn gives birth to irresistible hope. David has screwed up big time, but there *is* a way back to God – and he wants to show us the way. Each step of this journey is painful, but if we're willing to rise to the challenge and follow his lead, strong grace will sustain us and epic joy awaits.

Don't miss the direction of David's first step: he moves *towards* God, not *away* from Him. This is a perfect picture of what true repentance looks like, yet it flies in the face of our most primal human instinct when we feel shame: to run away and hide, just as Adam and Eve did.[9] David, though, responds to his grievous offences by throwing himself onto God for mercy because of His 'unfailing love' and 'great compassion' (v. 1). David humbly acknowledges God's good character and, by way of shameful comparison, his own fallen nature. He is a man marked by iniquity and transgression (vv. 1–2), sinful from conception (v. 5), evil in God's sight (v. 4) and persistently corrupt (v. 3).

However, perhaps the most striking lyric is David's confession, 'Against you, you only, have I sinned' (v. 4). Pause for a moment and let that sink in. David had slept with Uriah's wife and put her husband to death, yet he considers his sin to be primarily against God. Is that not outrageous?! Yes it is, but herein lies the key to truly grasping the glorious scandal of God's grace. So often we view our sin in purely horizontal terms – how it affects ourselves and those around us – but this means that our forgiveness must also be found horizontally, and that poses a problem.

> *...he considers his sin to be primarily against God. Is that not outrageous?!*

Consider David's dilemma here: if his sin was

primarily against Bathsheba and Uriah, then he would have had to turn to them for mercy. We are not told whether Bathsheba ever forgave David, but even if she did, what about Uriah? Could he forgive from beyond the grave? Of course not! David could never hear the words 'I forgive you' from the mouth of the man he had murdered. Therefore, if he was ever going to be free of the guilt of betrayal and bloodshed, David would need to find forgiveness from elsewhere. But where?

The beauty of David's confession is that he shifts the focus away from himself and the horizontal consequences of his sin and lifts his eyes to the Merciful One. Does this mean that David had not sinned against Bathsheba and Uriah? Of course not. David, however, rightly acknowledges that his sin was first and foremost an act of violent insurgency against the holiness of God, breaking both His law and His heart. David was guilty of cosmic treason, therefore pardon could only be obtained vertically from the Most High God.

We can learn so much from David here about how to deal with sin – he doesn't sugarcoat it, deny it or try to justify it, rather he simply steps up and owns it. Is that what you do with your sin? David knew that coming clean was the only way of becoming clean, therefore his humble confession is followed accordingly by bold petition.

As a father of four, it never ceases to amaze me how often my kids get themselves into all kinds of mess. It's as if they are magically, magnetically drawn towards anything and everything that could get them caked in crud: mud, blood, ketchup, cowpats … you name it! However, what they are not so good at is cleaning themselves up afterwards – that joyous duty normally falls to me or their mum. In a similar way, while David recognises that he is solely responsible for the sin that had soiled his soul, he also readily acknowledges that he cannot clean himself up. Therefore, like a child, he comes to his Father and effectively asks for a bath. Note the phrases that David uses in the opening verses: 'blot out my transgressions' (v. 1); 'Wash away all my iniquity' (v. 2); 'cleanse me from my sin' (v. 2). David is filthy and he knows that only God can make him clean. But how could this happen? David tells us in verse 7: 'Cleanse me with hyssop, and I shall be clean; wash me, and I shall be whiter than snow.'

The Hebrew word here for 'cleanse' is stronger than that used in verse 2 – it speaks of being deeply, thoroughly purged. David fully believes that his dirty heart can be washed as white as snow, the key to his confidence being found in his reference to hyssop. This common herb is mentioned only a handful of times in the Bible. In Exodus 12 God's people were instructed to use hyssop to smear the blood of a sacrificed lamb onto the doorposts of their homes, thus causing the angel of death to pass over them.[10] In other words hyssop was synonymous with salvation. It was also used by priests in various cleansing rituals,[11] so hyssop was synonymous with purity too.

The king's plea to be cleansed with hyssop is therefore loaded with meaning, but it is also pregnant with promise. One thousand years later David's great descendent, the man Jesus Christ, would enter the scene. As the merciful Son of God was mercilessly nailed to a Roman cross, he was offered wine vinegar to drink, held up to him on a hyssop branch by soldiers. Here we see the fulfilment of what David had seen through the eyes of faith: Jesus, the Lamb of God was slaughtered so that rebels could be purified from the stain of sin[12] and delivered from the penalty of death. Jesus was punished for David's crimes so that David could be washed clean. The cross literally was a bloodbath, as William Cowper so graphically put it:

There is a fountain filled with blood,

Drawn from Immanuel's veins,

And sinners plunged beneath that flood

Lose all their guilty stains.[13]

What are the guilty stains polluting your life right now? Whatever they are, the only agent potent enough to permanently remove them is the blood of Jesus because 'the blood of Jesus … purifies us from all sin' (1 John 1:7). If you want to get rid of the toxic residue of sin in your life, you need to follow David's example. Turn to Jesus and confess your mess, for: 'If we confess our sins, he is faithful and just and will forgive us our sins and purify us from all unrighteousness' (1 John 1:9).

David begins his petition with a plea for cleansing, but as he progresses down the path of repentance, he recognises that it isn't only forgiveness he needs; he requires a complete overhaul: 'Create in me a pure heart, O God and renew a steadfast spirit within me', (v. 10) he cries. Sin has literally wrecked David's life and so he turns to the only One who can put it back together again.

However, his petition doesn't end there. David continues: 'Do not cast me from your presence or take your Holy Spirit from me' (v. 11). The presence of God, once so precious to David, had been the furthest thing from his mind as he defiled Bathsheba and devoured her husband. But now, as he turns back to God and confesses his sin, he isn't content to merely receive God's mercy; he wants to revel in His presence again. Do not miss either the connection between this verse and the line that follows: 'Restore to me the joy of your salvation' (v. 12). As we saw in the opening chapter, God's presence and God's joy are inextricably linked.

I love this lyric so much because David absolutely understands the fact that true salvation is experiential. Frankly, he wants his joy back! As the psalm passes its halfway mark, David begins to thrill at the memory of what his life used to be like before Bathsheba, before bloodshed, before disgrace. He casts his mind back to the glory days when the joy of God's presence incited him to dance deliriously through the streets of his city with nothing but an ephod and the grace of God to cover his shame. He would worship with such infectious ferocity that the multitudes were swept up in ecstasy with him. And then the penny drops: his best days do not have to be behind him; it *can* be like that again!

Maybe this is resonates with you because, like David, you really blew it at some point and have endured a joyless Christian existence ever since. If that is the case, then with all the love in my heart I want to hold out to you this beautiful truth: God's grace *is* bigger than your sin. When you view your transgression through the lens of the cross, faith will rise and joy will feel attainable again.

David's journey back to joy is now gathering pace. As his stride lengthens, he starts to see beyond the prison bars of his own selfish desires and subsequent self-loathing. Indeed as he dares to dream of a fresh start marked by a pure heart, a willing and steadfast spirit and unbridled joy, things begin to look different. People are no longer viewed as objects to be used and abused, but rather as precious souls to be served, saved and lovingly led: 'Then I will teach transgressors your ways, so that sinners will turn back to you' (v. 13).

Note that David has now moved on from petitioning God and has started making big promises. Rather than lustful kisses and devious lies, David will once again use his mouth to teach, sing and declare God's praise (vv. 14–15). Like a beggar who has just been given the keys to the royal parlour, David is now devoted to calling other beggars to join him at the banquet. He has received lavish grace and wants to lavishly distribute it to others. Similarly, rather than burnt offerings, David now places himself on the altar, giving all that he has left: a broken spirit and contrite heart (vv. 16–17). It begs the question what would … could … should your life look like after an encounter with the transforming grace of God?

As we reach the end of the psalm, there is no doubt that David is a changed man. Every step of his journey has been gruelling, but the bones that God, in his gracious purposes, crushed are now ready to rejoice. The king who once danced so passionately before the ark is about to make a comeback. His guilty feet might have lost their rhythm, but now – having walked the road of repentance – they're itching to hit the dance floor once more, and David knows exactly what track he wants the DJ to play ...

Ecstasy – sin covered

4

We all have a tune that makes us jump up and dance our heart out – at least we should have! Mine is 'Shake your body' by Shy FX & T-Power. As a DJ I found it was always guaranteed to get the place bouncing. It was therefore the only tune that I stipulated *had* to be on the set list when I got married.

If King David had a jump-up track, it was probably Psalm 32. His raw, reflective lament, Psalm 51, might well have been written in a melancholic minor key, but there is no question that his pulsating follow-up number, Psalm 32, is a cheerful, major key masterpiece. Check it out:

Psalm 32

Of David. A maskil.[14]

Blessed is the one
    whose transgressions are forgiven,
    whose sins are covered.
Blessed is the one
    whose sin the LORD does not count
    against them
    and in whose spirit is no deceit.

When I kept silent,
    my bones wasted away
    through my groaning all day long.
For day and night
    your hand was heavy on me;
my strength was sapped
    as in the heat of summer.

Then I acknowledged my sin to you
    and did not cover up my iniquity.
I said, 'I will confess
    my transgressions to the LORD.'
And you forgave
    the guilt of my sin.

Therefore let all the faithful pray to you
    while you may be found;
surely the rising of the mighty waters
    will not reach them.
You are my hiding-place;
    you will protect me from trouble
    and surround me with songs of deliverance.

I will instruct you and teach you in the way
you should go;
    I will counsel you with my loving eye on you.
Do not be like the horse or the mule,
    which have no understanding
    but must be controlled by bit and bridle
    or they will not come to you.
Many are the woes of the wicked,
    but the Lord's unfailing love
    surrounds the one who trusts in him.

Rejoice in the Lord and be glad, you righteous;
    sing, all you who are upright in heart!

It is widely agreed by Bible scholars that both Psalm 51 and Psalm 32 are linked to the same shameful episode in David's life: the Bathsheba files. However, while Psalm 51 is an impassioned plea *for* mercy from the grimy depths of guilt, Psalm 32 is a riotous celebration *of* mercy from the glorious heights of grace. The cry of David's heart had been for God to rekindle the joy of His salvation and Psalm 32 is the conclusive evidence that God gladly answered that prayer.

David launches the psalm by painting a stunning word picture of a man who is blessed. The Hebrew word that he uses here for 'blessed' can also be translated 'happy'. In other words David has discovered the key to the treasure trove of true happiness and he wants to spread the wealth. His new-found joy is grounded in knowing that his sin has been forgiven, his shame has been covered and the charges against him have been dropped (vv. 1–2). He contrasts the image of this blessed man with that of an exhausted man who has been crushed, sucked of strength and robbed of joy (vv. 3–4). The David of Psalm 51 was wretched, racked with guilt and badly broken, whereas the David of Psalm 32 is restored, revelling in grace and blessed beyond measure.

But how did such a remarkable transformation occur? How did the king recover his joy? Helpfully,

David sums it up for us in verse 5:

> … I acknowledged my sin to you
>
> > and did not cover up my iniquity.
>
> I said, 'I will confess
>
> > my transgressions to the Lord.'
>
> And you forgave
>
> > the guilt of my sin.

David glances in the rear-view and reminds us of his painful confession and humble repentance. However, it is the phrase 'I … did not cover up my iniquity' that really stands out when considered alongside an earlier line: 'Blessed is the one … whose sins are covered.' David is clearly ecstatic that his sin has been covered, yet he is also emphatically certain that it was not him who did the covering? So how were David's heinous crimes 'covered'?

In Psalm 51 David placed his faith for forgiveness in the future finished work of Jesus, who John the Baptist describes as 'the Lamb of God, who takes away the sin of the world!' (John 1:29). We've already seen that the blood of the cross cleanses the putrid stains of sin, but Jesus came to do even more than that, He came to remove the guilt of sin by taking it with Him into the bowels of the grave. David's sin was covered because it was buried with Christ in the tomb and left there to rot. That's how God covers sin. He doesn't merely sweep it under the carpet; He does away with it decisively, emphatically, permanently, eradicating every trace of disgrace. I love how the prophet Micah puts it: 'You will … hurl all our iniquities into the depths of the sea' (Mic. 7:19).

David's sin was covered because it was buried with Christ in the tomb…

David was 100% forgiven, no longer haunted by guilt or plagued by regret, but rather purged on the inside and liberated from shame. There is no greater gift to receive, no sweeter freedom to savour than the salvation of God. It's little wonder then that King David described himself as so blissfully blessed. If a clean heart and full pardon was *all* that God had done for him, it would have been reason enough for David to put his party pants on and let loose. But, as is so often the case with God, there was yet more grace for David to savour, as we see in verse 7:

You are my hiding-place;
     you will protect me from trouble
and surround me with songs of deliverance.

Don't miss the magnitude of this verse. In Psalm 51 David petitioned, 'Do not cast me from your presence' (v. 11) because sin had so decimated his relationship with God and riddled him with anxiety and insecurity that he wondered if God would ever feel close, or even safe, again. But here in Psalm 32 David is in an altogether different place, no longer running and hiding *from* God in fear and shame, but rather running *to* and hiding *in* God in peace and safety. David's sin had been buried; now, like a rescued child, he finds himself in the warm embrace of a loving Father who, rather than scolding him, is singing deliverance songs over him. Take a moment to meditate on that …

What a staggering picture of redeeming grace this is. What hope it offers to all those of us who know only too well the terror and trauma of sin in our lives. As we marvel at this miracle, it is crucial that we recognise that David's journey back to joy was about so much more than merely seeking God's forgiveness for the foul things he had done. David was undoubtedly jubilant that his sins were covered, but ultimately the pinnacle of his joy was a restored relationship with God. He didn't simply want forgiveness; he wanted the Father. More than God's pardon he craved God's presence, where true joy is found. David rejoiced in salvation, but supremely he found joyful rest in the arms of the Saviour. This is a great challenge to us as Christians in a consumeristic culture where we are so often tempted to prize the gift above the giver. As we consider David's epic journey back to joy, let's be in no doubt that it was *who* not *what* was waiting for him at the end that mattered most.

Once God gets his man firmly back in His gracious grip, He grabs the microphone from David's hand and drops a few lyrics of his own. In verses

It's as if God is saying to David, 'Don't get it twisted – you need me more than they need you, so stay close!'

8–9 God promises that He will once more coach David and tenderly lead him down the right paths, so long as he remains humble, teachable and devoted. This promise is particularly poignant when considered alongside David's resolution in Psalm 51 to teach transgressors God's ways (v. 13). It's as if God is saying to David, 'Don't get it twisted – you need me more than they need you, so stay close!'

As the song draws to a close and David's journey nears its end, the king reflects on the tragedy of his own former wickedness and contrasts it with the ecstasy of his current state:

Many are the woes of the wicked,

but the Lord's unfailing love

surrounds the one who trusts in him.

There is no more secure place to be than resting and trusting in God, knowing that wherever you turn you are constantly surrounded on all sides by His unfailing love. David had tapped into the mind-blowing miracle of God's unstoppable, indestructible love – something that would enthral the Apostle Paul at a later date: 'For I am convinced that neither death nor life, neither angels nor demons, neither the present nor the future, nor any powers, neither height nor depth, nor anything else in all creation, will be able to separate us from the love of God that is in Christ Jesus our Lord' (Rom. 8:38–39).

David's love for God had failed significantly, but God's love for David had endured spectacularly. David is back where he truly belongs, and where he longs for us to be too. His rousing, closing words strike a very similar chord to those of the king who had once danced ferociously, freely through the streets of Jerusalem, so full of joy and love for his Lord that dignity and decorum completely deserted him: 'Rejoice in the LORD and be glad, you righteous; sing, all you who are upright in heart!' (v. 11). Once more David's passion for his God is burning so hot and bright that others are being drawn into the inferno of his praise. The king is again summoning worshippers to take to the streets and join him in the dance of the righteous.

> *David's love for God had failed significantly, but God's love for David had endured spectacularly.*

However, maybe you still feel that you have no right to join in such worship because you feel anything but righteous. Perhaps, like David, you have sinned grievously, even persistently, and so you would feel a hypocrite to now dance before the Lord. If that's you, let me encourage you one final time to look to Jesus. Consider the cross where 'God made him who had no sin to be sin for us, so that in him we might become the righteousness of God' (2 Cor. 5:21). Glimpse again the empty tomb where the risen Christ buried every trace of our sin so that we no longer need to bear the shame of it. It is Jesus who gladly makes us righteous, upright and accepted, and He does so by grace – sheer grace alone.

Perhaps, like David, you have sinned grievously, even persistently, and so you would feel a hypocrite to now dance before the Lord.

None of us deserve to dance and sing and celebrate and know joy in our lives, but King David has shown us that there is a journey that will lead us back to joy. The glory of the gospel is that the greater our filthiness, the greater our forgiveness and the more grateful our praise. The more we pour out our confession before the Lord, the more He will flood our lives with His mercy. The deeper our repentance, the sweeter our rejoicing will be. So I implore you:

TURN TO JESUS TODAY.
Confess your sin.
Embrace His grace.
Then dance for joy with all your might!

Notes

Introduction

1 http://news.bbc.co.uk/1/hi/
world/europe/1433713.stm

2 Matt. 28:20.

1. Tragedy – sin committed

3 See Jesus' parable about the
lost son (Luke 15:11–32).

2. Agony – sin exposed

4 John 1:5.

5 Matt. 5:14.

6 Ps. 119:105.

7 Rom. 2:4.

3. Humility – sin confessed

8 The ESV and other versions of
the Bible translate this title as
'the choirmaster'.

9 Gen. 3:8.

10 Ex. 12:22–23.

11 Lev. 14 and Num. 19.

12 John 1:29.

13 William Cowper, 'There is a
Fountain' (1772).

4. Ecstasy – sin covered

14 'Maskil' is probably a literary
or musical term.

a division of **10**ofthose.com

10Publishing is the publishing house of **10ofThose**.

It is committed to producing quality Christian resources that are biblical and accessible.

www.10ofthose.com is our online retail arm selling thousands of quality books at discounted prices. We also service many church bookstalls and can help your church to set up a bookstall. Single and bulk purchases welcome.

For information contact: **sales@10ofthose.com**

or check out our website: **www.10ofthose.com**